At the Storm's Edge

Palewell Press

At the Storm's Edge

Poems – Frank McMahon

At the Storm's Edge

First edition 2020 from Palewell Press,
www.palewellpress.co.uk

Printed and bound in the UK

ISBN 978-1-911587-30-9

The cover design is Copyright © 2020 Camilla Reeve

The front cover photo is Copyright © 2020 Sheridan Reeve

The back cover photo is Copyright © 2020 Frank McMahon

A CIP catalogue record for this title is available from the British Library.

Acknowledgements

"Berlin 1933" was published on-line by *I am not a silent poet* and *The Poet by Day*

"Shoes" was published on-line by *The Poet by Day, I am not a Silent Poet* and *Persona Non Grata*

"Universal Credit" was published by *Riggwelter* and *I am not a Silent Poet*

"First Cast" was published on-line by *The Poet by Day*

"Evolution" was published in *The Cannon's Mouth* and *Cirencester Scene*

"Finding Tyndale at Nibley" was broadcast on *Corinium Radio* and published in *Cirencester Scene*

"Wordsmiths" was published in *The Curlew* and *The Poet by Day*

The Cannon's Mouth published: "On the Hill", "Château de Minerve", "A Lark Ascends", "Seven Springs", "Early Morning Frost", "Night Shift", "Christina's World", and "Flint"

"Night Shift" was also published by *Brittlestar* and *Cirencester Scene*

The following poems appeared on-line in *The Poet by Day*: "Seven Springs", "Quiet City", "A Cage of Shadows", "Ambiguous Spring", "I am a Citizen", "What Use?" and "Pebble"

"Equivocation" was published by *I am not a Silent Poet*

"New Home" and "Survival of an Artist" were published by *Cirencester Scene*

"Family Gathering" was broadcast on *Corinium Radio*

Dedication

Dorothy

Anna and Jonathan

Mark and Ione

Sam, Tom and Dora

Orla, Briony and Agatha

And with Special Thanks to:

Somewhere Else Writers, Cirencester

Rona Laycock

Jamie Deedes (The Poet by Day)

Contents

LAY OUT THE BODIES

Berlin 1933

Find the glass window set in the cobbles
outside Humboldt's University. You'll
need to angle your view and wait until
the light reveals the whiteness of the empty
shelves, a void in Europe's heart.
Judischen, entartate. This is where
they began the burning of the books,
flames and sparks, yellow like stars, lighting the way
to ghettos, wagons, lines of wire, ashes, bones.

Ghosts gather, tug at your sleeve politely,
plead that you read the Book of the Dead.
Its opening page lies at your feet. Descend
to lamentation's rainbow.

Shoes

Shoes, pointing in all directions
as if they could not decide which
way to go. Ahead the river,
wide and fast, its shore empty of boats.
And people. The shoes, fissured,
soiled, heels broken; children's clogs. As

they stood in their final sunlight:
prayers? Huddles of comfort? Piss and
shit leaking onto ancient leather.
Hurled backwards, no funeral flowers
save the smoke curling from the guns,
downwards, where the Duna receives
them, cold, reddening as it flows,
mere dross and cargo. A flask of
spirits opened, a cigarette
lit, safety catches on, the world
more Judenfrei.
                          Shoes, now again
pointing in all directions.

Château de Minerve

Cathar village, invested once with hope
and simple faith until professed belief
was burned out of their bodies
and ashes scattered on a ravaged land.

Deep rooted vines produced a richer wine
before the river, drop by drop,
uncovered desiccation.

No record when it began to lose itself,
prayers for revival futile
while the wine turned sour
in the dwindling cellars.

Engraved stones beneath
a scorching sun.

De Profundis

Dragged gagged and wordless down to the heart
of the unforgiving maw. Hands push her
through and slam the door; the key
is turned and bolts slid home. She stands

still, her eyes soaking up darkness.
Sounds fade to silence. Odours linger
of body sweat and spittle.
She tries to store them,

objects from beyond. She moves,
a maimed crab in a sea of ink,
along the floor, leftwards always
leftwards, fingers as eyes. A bed, perhaps

a bench, nothing else but the rough
stone of every wall until she finds again
the door. Time stops for her now,
no way of counting but through heartbeats.

Into the keyhole she whispers her name.

Rope

Each day it took a little longer.
Survival's trap. She carried the bucket
to the well once more, tied the rusting
handle, turned the windlass slowly.
The rope uncoiled, uncoiled
until she heard the whisper of metal
entering water. Familiar odours of damp earth
as red dust flustered round her face.

A groan, a groan repeated as she turned
the splintered handle, fighting the weight,
conserving every drop.
It was when she dipped her hands
to rinse her face, it was when
she stumbled that the bucket fell.
Untethered.

Heat tightened its bands around her head.
She shut her eyes against the coruscating light,
turned, listened for the sound
of an ox-cart on the road, footsteps
of a child returning; imagined a neighbour
bringing a replacement.

The rope hung limp.

Nameless

Along the highways and the sea lanes
of the empires, lay out the bodies of those
who died of unnatural causes: wars,
famine, indenture, slavery, neglect.
Itemise the treasures and the spoils
wrenched from the planet's abdomen.
Then count and if you can,
calculate the profit for each corpse.
Easier to hide behind the bottom line,
the balance sheet of the infinite unknown.
Though it starts, as always,
with one man in a mine hawking
his bloodied lungs against a dripping wall.

A Cage of Shadows

I can't get out, can't get out, can't,
If I could did where would I go?

Not the park
not like that when, not even in a gang,
too rubbish for the rubbish kids.

I can't break the glass all covered in crap
to let out the smell of skank on my bed
to light up the corners
where I crouched and cowered
to shout to someone out there.

If I could did where would I go?
Not the station,watch the trains
come and go come and go

people rushing like ferrets for the last train home;
can't go there might walk along the track
in the dark find a place to.

All of us kids bags of human shit
in the arsehole of our family.
Say it again yeah again
whack the words into our ears.
Dreams like hooks and blades.
I can't push back the clouds,
get through the memories, not like photos
you can't burn 'em not even with acid.

Get out if I could get out
find the river find the river tomorrow
boats, dead birds floating
I'd be a tide watched stared at useful
moving who knows where but moving.

In the Gulag

A crippled man, eight floors up, the lift
broken again. A woman, bed-bound,
her harassed carers late once more while she
hazes in a dream of rotting fruit.

Homeless citizens fly-tipped
to alien towns or camped
beneath the underpass; others
filling night-time doorways.

Third child, non-child!
Third child, non-child!
Should have thought of that
before…!
Just join the food-bank queue.

Better like this, no need
for wire or watchtowers,
the rabid press as guard-dogs
of the dark and scattered places,
our gulag of wilful degradation.

Universal Credit

Learn this lesson: assume the supplicant's
position, low before the arbiter.
Hang your petition on the ox's horn and
pray as it turns and plods inside the keep.
Forty-two days in the wilderness, longer
than Christ's self-chosen stay. Time to go home
and count the copper pennies in your palm, time
to scour the bins for corn cobs overlooked,
scraps on bones, nubs of bread, hide candles
and kindling, beg remission on your rent.
Time to forage hedgerows, scrape bark for baking
bread, claw the furrows for potatoes, hush
the hungry child while you lie clamped and clemmed,
fashioning hope from feathers and dung.

You may be lucky: beneficence
parsimonious may be granted or
day on day on days delays will find you
in winter's shadow outside the castle walls.

I am a citizen

I am a citizen of no country who
welcomes those whom war flings on our shores,
who feeds the last survivor, who wishes
he could staunch the blood of every wound,
could seal forever underground the chariots,
the spears lusting for others to impale.

I am a citizen of no country who
cries as the planet dies, writhes in toxic shock,
is gouged and burned to mute surrender.

I was called a citizen of no nation
when I went beyond our coasts to speak
of common ground, to learn their hopes
and history from their flags,
                              it seems that
I betrayed our flag, my kith and kin. I
should have stayed at home and drawn the blinds,
watched, instead, the fatuous retreat
to the towers on the cliffs, the hill forts,
their beacon fires sputtering in the rain.

We are citizens of the world,
though raised upon our native soils.
We will not permit you to partition our humanity.

It is the Sound

of a child abandoned on a hillside
of a man's tears falling across a rock
of a seabird caught in a trough of oil
of a whale lost amongst the throb of engines
of a mother pleading for the life of her child.

It is a sound
drawn from wet, wind-hammered fells
drawn from the curlew's piping
and the lapwing's winter cry
drawn from the farmer robbed of his fields
drawn from the tribes driven into exile
drawn from a saw cutting bone.

It is a sound distilled
from the edge of extinction
from war's obliteration
from the driving out of mercy.

It is sound that grinds against the skin
that lacerates the heart
but is not heard by all and so it must be amplified
a threnody for the loss of hope
played by the last surviving piper.

LOVE'S
COMPLICATIONS

First Cast

An island without water.
We rose just after dawn,
this summer of endless sun and strawberries,
unmoored the boat, began to work the oars.
Steady lift splash pull, lift splash pull,
'til we could drift mid-fjord.
One simple line and spinner.
Wait as sweat dries; salt, silence then sharp tug,
resistance against the filament drawn in.
First fish! Slither of silver and black. And on and on
as mackerel filled the boat around our feet.
Much easier this than working out love's complications,
shimmer and wonder lifting me beyond
my youthful self-absorptions.

Evolution

It takes a big leap of the imagination
to see the line of descent from dinosaur to blackbird,
until you view the fossil record.
But you still can't quite collapse fifty million years
into an hour's time-frame. Think then instead of falling
in love and being in love. Falling, but more crucially,
being caught in passion's net, held or trapped depending,
two tyros learning their moves on high-wire
or trapeze, diving earthwards, hands outstretched. Maybe
love really begins when both of them discard the net.

One Life

Can we imagine self, en-tubed, inert,
all drive and pleasure shrivelled to a husk?
Should love and duty first declare an end
to liberate the living from that stern

choice? Who can really know what lives within
a stricken frame? Who can breach the silent wall
behind which move our fantasies and plans?
Can we predict the moment when we'll know

that all our restless work is at an end?
Life insists on life, its metronomic
pulse day on day demanding that we tend
our duties and the offices of love.

Earth or fire attend. Accept with grace
and wit. Last breaths can wait. And memory.

Homage

The day did not start well. Dave nearly
broached the yacht and Dave (the other one)
down in the galley was dodging pots
and flying pans. Order and sanity
restored we headed out, that Scottish dawn,
to journey to the Hebrides.
      The sea, quiet at first, began to grow,
usurping sky, piling higher than the mast,
bearing us up then down into its troughs.
We held our breath, feeble in its undulating rhythm,
poised in fear of the breaking, overwhelming
crests, in silent prayer. But we climbed smooth
and slid again, learning to work with
the water's pulse and flow.
      My father would have smiled at this.
Wartime convoy service, Arctic and Atlantic,
torpedoed nearly to extinction.
He only spoke about it once.
It was enough.

Family Gathering

This is where we've met,
where landscape offers space.

"Quick, quick, you can't catch me!"
Oh yes I can, with cunning.
I know where the flower beds narrow.
You'll never escape me there.
Unless I pretend.
I'll pretend.

"Play hide and seek? Count to ten then,
no fifteen!" They'll find me by water,
gazing on pondweed, deadly green
like Sunday afternoons when clocks dragged their
feet, ticking echoes of the morning's sermon.
Wildly we emitted raw blasts of turbulence,
braced to pay the consequential price
for breaking Sunday's peace.

Aspens whisper, braid the breeze
between their leaves, rumour rain.
Elderberries beaded like drops
from a verdant sky. Squall of rooks
crashes from the clustered woods.

"Sorry, I was." Somewhere between,
somewhere between."Here, let me show
you this sunflower, yellow-headed diva,
admitting with grace the butterflies
to hover and partake."

Tree house is clattering with chatter,
explosive ululations. Who is really listening
and does it really matter
as long as they can have these moments
of unguarded light?

Wren's ostinato fades to quiet
in the stillness of the birch.
Scrolls of pure white bark, nicks,
music-box notes, ships plotted on radar,
heading where?

          Futures,
mid-life, pondered in currents
of easy conversation. And ours?
as we drift our hands through
lavender and rosemary.
Passion and remembrance jostle,
loss and history, the past imperfect.
Old questions niggle still, leading where?
Simpler to pick apart a teasel
piece by piece.

Hungry calls distract.
"Wait, look how they sway and bow,
these reeds, courtiers before the kingcups.
Yellow is the colour of homage today.
Do you wear yellow? No
but you are pardoned. Eat!"

/continued

Follow the shafts of light:
scarlet rosehips, crimson plums,
dusted blue by night moths' wings,
first blush on apples
skimped by drought.

House wall, solid
but evidence of slip and restitution,
infill and making do.

Present and future,
intertwined, pulsing together.
Let them run on and on,
this day, these days.

Young Voices

Young voices carolling Christmas,
hovering round the petals of each note.
Give them time and they'll reach perfect
pitch deep in the purple stamen,
grow stronger for when they start to build
their life on what we have bequeathed.

Take for inspiration wild flowers,
survivors of fire and ice,
at home in desert sands, crevices and verges,
meadowlands and swamps, heedless
of borders, a chorale of every colour,
harmony building from harebell and rose.

Allotment

Hefting water out of the river
to feed the newly-planted.
Long years since I had to do the same on Uncle's farm:
white enamel bucket hanging from a windlass,
sweet water drawn from deep. I could only lift a half
a pailful then. Brothers, neighbour's girls,
rudimentary washes after endless play;
earth closet in the yard, potatoes,
their skins slowly curling in the cauldron
on the hearth. Somewhere a clock. Bored one day,
I stood beside the well and bawled for help.
Dad came running and rough chastisement
was love's affirmation.

Barely a check before I swooshed
down the hay bales in the barn, innocent
until the straws in my hair betrayed me.
The years have added muscle, as I bend
and dip and heave from the grateful water,
remembering my boyhood's guilty smile.

Board Games

Waves of laughter wash across the oilcloth-
covered table, chaff and chiding as we plod
through Dingbats like some boot-sucking bog,
beating our brains as we fathom inscrutable clues,
enduring its attrition for these moments.

A Seaman's Pouch

R166216
Lost, replaced, now traced at last,
my father's.
Neat cursive script in different hands,
no wasted words:
ships, dates, evaluations,
a carpenter in a world
of steel and water.

Winnipeg2, chartered once by Pablo Neruda
to take from France Spanish refugees
and carry them to Chile.
"The critics may erase all of my poetry if they want
But this poem, that today I remember,
nobody will be able to erase"

Convoy ON-139
A line of life stretched taut
and fear haunts each keel.
Curse/bless the storm pounding
against the knuckled rivets;
pray that the head grinding
down against the crushing walls,
pray that the head will rise and breathe,
pray that the engines will not fail,
pray you will not be lost
in the ocean's wrack.

22/10/1942
U-443, Wolf Pack Puma.
This line of life, men and cargo,
war, time and water intersect
and Winnipeg2 is doomed.

49°,51' North, 27°,58'West
Two sudden blows.
The pictures show a ship in a gentle ocean,
scuppers nearly under water, men in lifeboats.
I magnify and peer, hoping I will see him
but I know I won't because.

21.48. The line of life, a shipmate
who saw he wasn't there,
who went below, hefted him
over his shoulder. Four days unconscious,
a wife now knowing where or how he was.

Only once he talked about what he had seen and heard,
annihilating seas and storms, men burning in oil.

A father's pouch,
discharged from life
with honour.

THE UNDERTOW OF GRIEF

On the hill

Tell me again. Why did I come here?
Was I invited? And if I was
who by? And if they said they'd come
why am I here alone?

Every path is clear
no mist concealing beast
or man or their approach.
Or woman.

The hill falls away to a copse
of oaks and the sky rises
to a kestrel's flight. Hover.
Watch as the sun's glow catches
the steeple of the church.

Turn and turn in a slow
unsteady circle round
the compass of this hill.
Turn and turn again
as a sob echoes
in the hollow of the wind.

Pebble

I choose a pebble from the beach
and lick a fleck of salt
from the red/brown round. Pebble
to cherish through this journey. Grit

and strength and wit must all combine
to carry out this pledge. Northwards.
Find the first hill. Grief lies
beyond evasion and finds me in moments

of repose between fell and crag,
peat bog and flooding stream.
Two hundred miles, one sea left behind,
the other found. Sunlight then spindrift,

one last steep hill falling between the red-tiled
homes to the flat, grey sea. A membrane bursts,
spilling everything distilled:
sorrow and ache and pride. Jolted,

I gasp and clutch a rail. Salt burns my cheek.
Walk, walk to meet the sea.
I place the pebble on my boot. A wave inspects
and takes its tribute. I turn and climb, talking
again in silence to one unseen.

Limestone

It seizes me again, the undertow of grief,
there on the limestone pavement. Days
of walking and exertion, when in a moment
of repose, it surges over me and drags.
I sit on the limestone blocks,
moulded over centuries and hollowed, grain
after grain by the winter's rain and frost.

So we are being shaped, our family
bereft. No point scanning the horizon
for what cannot be realised, yet still I persist,
describing the larks startling me with song,
the buzzard haunting the copse of trees,
the wild flowers' colours by the stream.
She carries our love, which can only flower
now in what we give each other.

Elegies

1.
The radio was silent, no paper
bought or other media sought
to bring the world's disasters and concerns.
We had our own news,
grief beyond bearing, borne
by those who could endure them least.
Blackness filled our windows and
hid the moon and stars.
That morning, we breakfasted on thorns.

2.
We were all ready, our homes and our
imagined worlds, waiting to give you,
day by day and year on year, the best
of our imperfect selves, to watch you
climb the branches of our love
and catch the world's excitement.
But you were overwhelmed.

Yet you will voyage with us,
there in every season, learning all the steps
of your childhood's dance.

Royalty

For Bryan Southwell

You were the King, upbraided in rehearsal
for taking too long to die. "They'll all miss
the last bus home if you don't speed this up!"
Even now, your fury reverberates.

Ah, my gracious friend, so many miles walked
upon the links, everything elegant,
even your bon mots in the midst of our
vulgar chaffing. The Schubert Impromptus

as we drove those Norfolk byways, the sun
flecking the chestnut leaves. The Canterbury
Tales in Melton, shared hours of bawdiness
and helpless laughter. You could have graced those

boards, making love to the Wife of Bath
and who knows else.
                  Admissions and discharges, blow
after vicious blow, cries of pain filling
the ward, nothing imagined for effect.

In the end, death could not come soon enough.
You slipped away, into the wings, denying
us all one final curtain call. You were
ready, not us, no, palms uplifted, empty.

Midnight Calls

The spool replayed will not erase.
Hard frost can stop it dead. Or anything unbidden,
so you must step again inside those frames

and hear once more those midnight calls,
your heart imploding for you know
(the spool replayed will not erase,)

that you must pack a case, scrape ice,
find the reassurance of white lines
(for you must step again inside those frames,)

search solace in each other's clouded silence
until you find a door unlike any other.
The spool replayed will not erase.

Enter, cross a floor of shards, breathe air
churning with what cannot be voiced.
So you must step again inside those frames.

A tunnel opens, darkness floods across your eyes,
one hand to hold, one hand to feel ahead.
The spool replayed will not erase
so you must step again inside those frames.

Christina's World

after Andrew Wyeth

It rises now, that stifled cry of pain and I am bound
to look again and go beyond. And back.

That family then, in a nearby road,
large house, high ceilings,
beside the public park
where we could run at will;
their son, his home an iron lung,
beyond our boyhood's games.

If we had met and talked, there beneath
the lead-blue sky, seeing the pallid shadows
on the distant walls, the cart tracks through the grass,
where would my questions have begun?
With withered limbs? Your light pink dress
and sturdy shoes? The flow of wind and sun
across your face? Eyes, words, gestures? Looking now,

I infer a struggle wilfully engaged
in a landscape unconstrained, a looking-beyond
the brow of the curving hill, the gift of smaller steps,
a gathering–in of things, their inner brightness,
nothing too small to overlook,
the cussed discoveries of stillness.

Tagasode

Whose sleeves?
Not yours, I hope,
on any canvas.
My gawky hands
could never ply the brush
to paint the pegs or frame
where your clothes would hang:
silk dresses, Kashmir scarves,
not needed any more.

My fingers would be grasping
at the air
you filled and graced
until the last breath left.

Tagasode: classical Japanese wooden frame where one would hang clothes of a departed loved one, invoking memories.

Checking in

You've packed your bags and checked them in,
been processed through security,
bought some scotch at the duty-free,
then sit, a latte in your hand,
waiting for the final call to board.
When.

Your partner, family, friend exclaim:
The flight's delayed. How long?
Who knows? Then all the screens go blank.
People mill and swirl, bark down mobile phones,
hover for announcements.
You let it all wash round and wait for news.
There will be news, so just sit still.

Sit still. Sounds evaporate, eyes
evade the strident lights. Deeper
you drift as if drowsing on a beach
or by a pool. Some time, who knows when,
you feel the gentle pressure of a hand.
There is no noise, all screens are blank.
All travellers have gone. Save one.
Vaguely, someone's face.

SOMEWHERE
ANOTHER VOICE

What use?

I imagine the opposite, where poets break
their pens, clamp silence on their tongues,
where every line of verse has been erased:
blank pages, empty screens.

I imagine then a desert where remorseless
dunes have buried waterholes and trees,
where no one dares to irrigate or plant,
where the wind no longer carries voices.

What is a land without rain?
What is one voice against the censors
and the engineers of souls?

I sing because I must.
Somewhere a flower may bloom,
induce the implacable
to hesitate
as the words uncoil and move
through eye and ear to the heart,
to reconsider.

Somewhere another voice may sing
and another and another
and another and another.

The Trumpets Fade

Ee-aye-addio, we won the war!
Except we didn't, on our own.
Sure we stood firm and kept the flame
but that didn't fit the myth back then,

converting partial truth to martial myth
as the long retreat began
and we fell back to the older ways
of nullity and conflict. Alone

is a long place to stand
as the quayside crumbles in the rising sea.
Dispatch hawks and falcons
to scour the fields beyond the waves
haggle with eagles for dross and ranker meat
to drop on empty plates.

The old halls fill with promise
of fading dreams restored, no cost too high
to gather from the hedgerows the drapes
and tattered flags to hide
the broken glass and shattered doors.

We shrink inside a bell jar
left on a dusty shelf.

Telling Tales

Lift words from a page,
mould them into gestures
and steps across a stage;
search for the heart of truth
within their voices,
inflecting for sincerity,
shaping the curves of rhythm.
Rap upon the tympanum,
lead us out beyond the border
to be danced by the wind's spirit
and whirled within its spells.

Craftwork

We shuttle, like spiders,
between the fractured, anguished days
and the leap of the heart
in a transcendental moment,
weaving our threads in the sway
of wind and rain, patient
for the time when light
will play on the captured dew
and passers-by will pause
as we wait behind the curling leaf.

Finding Tyndale at Nibley

"In principio creavit Deus cælum et terram.
Terra autem erat inanis et vacua" **Genesis Chapter 1**

A field of wheat, sides squared and neatly hedged.
As we come close, no weeds or wild flowers,
orthodoxy ripening as it should.
We enter, leave the budding woods, then out,

onto the escarpment, his tower tall and stark.
Its apex bears a refulgent golden cross.
Nearby, felled timber, neat-stacked like faggots,
sufficient to incinerate thinkers

independent, heretics, men, women
seeking their single way towards God's words.
This was his boyhood's country, lived between
the Severn and these hills, open to the winds,

contrary, turbulent. Hard questions
grew amongst his learning, thorny,
provocative, answers concealed,
seeds in a husk of silence, nurtured later

in the thickets of deeper learning: Greek,
Hebrew, flowering in the glottal stops,
cadences and plosives of everyman's tongue.
The ploughboy reads his Bible, pausing

longer at the turning of each furrow.
Around us in the rough, demotic ground,
knapweed and ragwort, hemp agrimony,
campion, sorrel, vetch and burnet rose.

A Lark Ascends

To the memory of Ralph Vaughan Williams

I just don't understand how it was done,
the translation of sound to notes on a stave,
not even for one voice or solo flute.

But I grasp the drive to capture bird-song,
wind-howl and the cries of the bereaved,
to work; no slackening before death took you,

plans for weeks and months ahead, the only way
to face each day before the void. Melodies
drawn thread by gossamer thread.

I am in the meadows when I hear them played,
in the woodlands and the salt-marsh,
music arcing back to a vanishing world,

to its ancient taproots, free to willing listeners.
Our music teacher told us you had died.
Then all I knew was Greensleeves. Now

your music threads my clothes and weaves
its way into my dreams. When it is my turn to leave,
Elihu's Dance, blackbirds and larks will sing me home.

Wordsmiths

Letters inscribed in air; branches
write the seasons and their fickle
variations, shredding coherence
as they thresh and whine; blasts and rants
of leaves and barren seeds.

Gift of the wasp's gall: indelible
tales from the oak's heart and hearing;
grand hotel and shelter, shade
for transient languor. Acorn fall.
Sap retreats slow to reticence.

Meditation under rimed sky,
the hermit's calligraphy spread
across the crystal sheet, utterance
of promise laid in autumn's scatter.

The year turns; dew-varnished beech glints
with angled light. Decipher the forest's
library: curlicues unfurling
on spring-dancing branches, stickiness
and insect hum, in April's breeze
the Book of Kells unscrolling.

Missa Solemnis

1.
"Listen, God, I've really tried, four years chained
like a slave sentenced to the galleys, bent
almost to the breaking point to capture
the impossible. I've ransacked the best
of the past, gone beyond everything I've done,
harrowed my soul to exhaustion. So, please, Lord,
open my ears and tell me you approve."

2.
Look, here he is, beyond the noises
and voices of this world. He's tried to take
us to the mountain-top.
We've practised days on endless days. Thank God
he couldn't hear us, scraping like angry cats as we
searched for perfect pitch; singers gasping
like a cart horse at the end of every chorus.
And we're Vienna's best!
Like him, we've sweated fear, hidden
in the cellars from the guns, closed
our shutters on the wagons
dripping blood along the cobbles.
Like him we prayed for peace.

/ continued

3.
This music, it's like trying to imagine God
and this is judgement day for half the town's come here.
We'll fail but even that will bring him glory.
We start!
Oh, we play, demons in a storm,
thrumming with fear and vertigo
and joy, scaling the impossible.
You dare not catch your breath
in case you fall within the pause
and lose forever the sublime.

Mahler's Childhood

Sisters, brothers. Dead, their bodies taken out
through the door at the back while customers
clattered through the front to drink each other
stupid, nights of wildness, oblivious
to the crows pecking at the windowpanes.
He tries to stop his ears with other sounds,
bugle calls and birdsong
but death still ticks its ceaseless metronome.

Survival of an Artist

Four players fight and chase his demons,
thudding the triple hammer-blows,
night-time's terror, suitcase ready packed.
They scrape his twisted entrails across
their fretted strings, follow/lead him underground,
where all light is banished.
He hunts for sounds, hopes to remember,
share these naked moments.

The future bleeds away…

as we pick at old obsessions.
The past is now a home with many rooms,
space for those who hold a ticket for nostalgia.
For each a saggy armchair on a floor of empty cans;
loop on loop, the TV screen shows newsreels of the past;
paper walls and cling-film roof, tools abandoned
on the lawn where foxes prowl. Brewing in the cellar,
fantasies, stench, nightsoil.

Equivocation

Sweat rises from the ground, oozes
through my hair as I bend and lift
uprooted weeds from soft, dark soil.

I find a piece of bone. Elsewhere,
some other place or country,
I might have asked to whom it once belonged
and if beneath the shovel's edge, history
was repeating deadly claims upon the present?

The dead know all about equivocation,
denial, lines of remorseless logic.
Must they sing again their
their songs of lamentation
before we cease our fumblings
in the charnel-pit of words?

WHAT THE WINDS HAVE WEATHERED

To the river

This is where we came, here, to the river
for the first time, along the rutted path,
cowslips, bluebells crowding at its edge; past
the dandelion meadow, its pale-white
quilt of puffballs waiting to be blown and cast.

Together to the river to explore
vigorous and sinuous, limpid rills
and ripples, the glistening flow of water.
Beneath the cobalt sky, each moment
folding into itself the heat, intense upon our faces,
the stones' cool splash and spray,
shouts and birdsong; each uplifted stone
setting free the grains of memory, where we were
one time held, entranced, imagination's
captives in the bubble of our dreams.

Flint

Spat
out of the earth,
jet of viscous magma
shucked beyond the writhing coils of lava,
shocked into something foreign.
Coolness, a hardening from within, shape, edge
descending into new confusion,
shifts and jostlings.

Stillness.

How long before they started?
Soft blows, slithers, invisible accretions
all around, press of growing weight.

Stasis.

Faint tremors from below,
then hefted upwards
weight falling away.
New elements.
Jabs of heat, unsalted waters pummelling,
air scouring, clenched grip of chill
until thrown aside, left, lifted.

Blows, shards battered away, two edges
thinned, a hollowing, insertion of something pliable.
Losing, I gain a voice.
I am lifted now. I hover, quivering; I breach the air,
stop in shock; a shuddering heat and wetness
closes all around.

Wrenched, laid out, the soil
of a conquered land heaped over.

Seven Springs

Who knows where they have come from?
No summer rains to fill the limestone caverns,
no spring-time residue and yet
the tongues of water spread in new directions,
loosestrife by the water's edge; and willow herb.

Across a once-ploughed field,
mineral insinuation
feeding the tangled hedgerows and
forcing the flush of hawthorn's white.

Folded in dew, summer might bring berries;
fieldfare and redwing on winter's winds.

Early Morning Frost

Frost across the ground, a magpie
sits on the bare fretwork of an oak;
a shaft of sunlight warms my neck
and brightens, on the shrunken pond,
its meagre lid of rime.

Shifts, movements
in the ice-melt, a subtle agitation
of familiar patterns,
like roles recast in domestic spaces
boundaries contested and redrawn.

I move to gain another view,
folding what I see into silence.

Quiet City

Paris, Venice, Udaipur: noise, rainbow
glitter, sensory orgasmatrons yet
nothing called serenity or the bliss
of a child carefree on a swing.

Here is my city, patient work of seeds
and seasons, pink campion, knapweed
and hawkbit's yellow, filling the meadows'
edge around the solitary ash. High

ridge on a clear day, chalk or clay
underfoot. Silent. Watch the hawk's lift
and stoop to the clustered oaks, sheen
on clear spring water bubbling. Cross

an open field where the breeze lifts away
the bric-a-brac of cares and toils,
open and be filled with birdsong,
float in moments endless ethereal.

Night-Shift

New laundered linen, the duvet crinkling
as I slide beneath, the amber glow
of the night-light tints the ceiling. Slow, slow

as the day sheds its weights and toils and I
rise lighter through solipsistic dreams
to the clearing in the wood where the wind

has brought its hoard from the workings of the day:
dreck, scattered seeds, inconsequential
dust, slivers of precious stones, the objects now

of nocturnal sift, pannage and salvage.
Faint rustles of wing and fur as I float
under starlight. Morning dull and bleary

reveals the cleared field. Whatever was preserved
may be found perhaps in the archives
of the trees: haze, dabs of gathered light.

Connections

Did it start as we helped to build the stooks
of wheat, the terrier ratting in the furrows?
Or going with our uncle to the river's tongues,
to stand astride the narrow channels
pail in hand as the tide flowed out,
inviting fish to enter? Or the journey
early morning on the horse-drawn cart
to take the churns of milk to the gathering place?

Hands rooted in loamy soil, routed from farm
to garden, connections to necessities,
taken in like morning air
or stroke of wind on cheek, neural,
mycorrhizal symbiosis, budding now
in the beads of sweat and gathered fruit.

Ambiguous Spring

The colours were returning: pathfinder celandine,
yellow and rich as butter freshly-churned,
pale infantry of hellebore and crocus,
racy flights of blackthorn, early bees.

But a pelt of snow has caped the distant hills;
milk-white ice conceals. Now wind
shrives skin, uncorks a furl of rooks
to larrick in the heady draughts
while buzzards rise, their plangent calls
ringing through the air above the trees,
at ease in their hunting spirals or jousting,
perhaps, in early season foreplay.

How will they fare tomorrow
when gales will drum and thump
and a waterfall sweeps downwards from the sky?
I will sow seeds, drink tea, wait until
the storms have clawed their way beyond,
judge the wisest moment to emerge,
to steep my hands in earth's true wealth,
where sun and water have balanced
what the winds have weathered,
to sample, grit under finger nails, palms
dark-stained or smeared blue with clay,
to fondle the webbèd texture,
test, grain by grain, its tilth, sniff aromas
of leaf and loam, praise the work of worm
and microbe, frost and air, declare,
to no one in particular, the land is ready.

The M6 in December

Out of the dark, a heron, gliding
over the steel boxes, frantic,
night-lit, squabbling for square metres
on the black tarmac lanes. Brittle
endurance of feather, flesh and bone;
here, a few steady wingbeats,
gone, trailing speculations
as we inched homewards. The measure
of its life: does it still carry
ancestral memories of field or stream,
or country silence, pictures, scents?
Or is life now simply following
messages long ago encoded,
to navigate this drab urban smear,
to hunt within this smaller world,
its easy flight a dismissal of our capture.

Glaciers

Blocked arteries, almost furred
by accumulating snow,
graunching between mountains
before they calve or feed
the thirsty rivers. Sloth-pace,
certainty and reassurance.

An ice core is drilled, extracted,
read like ancient manuscript;
texts in bubbled air reveal
years lean and fat, clouds of volcanic
ash until the deep point of clathrate *
where time's record disappears.

Descend the moulin, a river is in spate. **

Did someone mark the moment,
when the last drop melted?
What follows now? Grass making its claim,
gentians, lichens, insects exploiting rock and nook?
Snow will fall and slough away,
a haemorrhage of history and future.

* *Clathrate is virtually the bottom layer in a glacier, a mix of ice and
very compressed air.*

** *Moulin is a bore hole in a glacier, created naturally by meltwater.*

New Home

Our new home sits on a tilting hill, peals
of bells hung from the passing clouds; night-time
music, notes filling the space between the stars,
rubato nudging the rings of Saturn.

At the Storm's Edge

At the storm's edge
always, never knowing if it will discharge
and overwhelm, or if it will relent,
recede as the season drags itself upstairs and round the cot.
Or the days may reverse to that moment sundered
between joy and shock, the seconds scattered
across the antiseptic floor, silence drowning
the other's cry.
                    Light aches on the newborn's face
in the muffled house. A ghost demands
its feed, forever probing at the teat
with blue, waxed lips, growing thin on dreams.
At the storm's edge there is always a prayer.

The ghost is clothed, in a shoe-box laid,
carried away, an exit to be registered.

FRANK MCMAHON - BIOGRAPHY

Frank McMahon was born and raised in Birkenhead, Merseyside. After graduating he began his career in Social Work/Welfare as a practitioner and manager, working for three Local Authorities, British Red Cross and ActionforChildren. He also served for nine years as a school governor.

His last full-time post was to set up and manage a SureStart Children's Centre. "There is nothing like working with and for young children. They constantly teach you to look at the world with fresh eyes and be open to new experiences."

He is married with two children and six grandchildren.

When not writing (plays, a novel, short stories and poems) he enjoys walking, (The Cotswolds are his new playground); his allotment (save for the weeds), golf, chess, travel, music, and counts himself fortunate to have some wonderful friendships.

He is a member of Somewhere Else Writers Group in Cirencester, whom he thanks for their patience in reading and critiquing his work. As part of that group, he works with Corinium Radio on programmes and plays.

PALEWELL PRESS

Palewell Press is an independent publisher handling poetry, fiction and non-fiction with a focus on books that foster Justice, Equality and Sustainability.

The Editor can be reached on enquiries@palewellpress.co.uk

Angela Carr Wordpress.

Lightning Source UK Ltd.
Milton Keynes UK
UKHW020618120522
402810UK00007B/168